Talking Dirty to the Gods

Also by Yusef Komunyakaa

Dedications & Other Darkhorses
Lost in the Bonewheel Factory
Copacetic
I Apologize for the Eyes in My Head
Toys in a Field
Dien Cai Dau
February in Sydney
Magic City
Neon Vernacular: New and Selected Poems
Thieves of Paradise
Blue Notes: Essays, Interviews and Commentaries
Pleasure Dome: New and Collected Poems

Talking Dirty to the Gods

Poems by

YUSEF KOMUNYAKAA

Farrar, Straus and Giroux

New York

FARRAR, STRAUS AND GIROUX
18 West 18th Street, New York 10011

Printed in the United States of America
Published in 2000 by Farrar, Straus and Giroux
First paperback edition, 2001

The Library of Congress has cataloged the hardcover edition
as follows:
Komunyakaa, Yusef.
    Talking dirty to the gods : poems / by Yusef
Komunyakaa.— 1st ed.
      p. cm.
    ISBN-13: 978-0-374-27255-5 (alk. paper)
    ISBN-10: 0-374-27255-7 (alk. paper)
    I. Title.

PS3561.O455 T35   2000
811'.54—dc21

                              00021277

Paperback ISBN-13: 978-0-374-52793-8
Paperback ISBN-10: 0-374-52793-8

Designed by Margaret M. Wagner

www.fsgbooks.com
    P1

Acknowledgments

Grateful acknowledgment is made to the following publications, in which some of these poems originally appeared: *Agni, The American Poetry Review, The Atlanta Review, The Atlantic Monthly, Barrow Street, Boulevard, Caliban, Common Knowledge, DoubleTake, Epoch, Field, Five Points, The Flying Dutchman, Harvard Review, The Illinois Review, Many Mountains Moving, Meridian, Michigan Quarterly, The Nation, Nerve, New England Review, The New Republic, The Paris Review, Phoebe, Poetry, Poetry International, Shenandoah, Slate, The Southern California Anthology, The Threepenny Review, TriQuarterly, Two Girls Review, Verse, VOLT, xconnect.*

Anthologies: *The American Voice: Anthology of Poetry; The Beacon Best of 1999: Creative Writing by Women & Men of All Colors; The Best American Poetry 1999, 1998; Cape Discovery: The Provincetown Fine Arts Workcenter Anthology; Contemporary American Poetry* (Poulin); *The KGB Bar Book of Poems; Power Lines: A Decade of Poetry from Chicago: Guild Complex.*

Contents

Contents

Contents

Talking Dirty to the Gods

Hearsay

Yes, they say if you shave a monkey
You'll find a pragmatist, the president
Of a munitions plant, a tobacco tycoon,
Or a manufacturer of silicone breasts

Who owns a medieval château
Decorated with Picasso's *Weeping Women*
& Madonna's underwear. Disguised
In silver-winged motorcycle boots,

He plucks a guitar with his teeth
& teaches the peacock songs to draw the hawk
To its nest. Injected with enough steroids
To supernova into an overnight

Star, he's the sperm bank's
Most valuable donor. But contrary
To what you may have heard, this
Bellerophon, he isn't a great lover.

Homo Erectus

After pissing around his gut-level
Kingdom, he builds a fire & hugs
A totem against his chest.
Cheetahs pace the horizon

To silence a grassy cosmos
Where carrion birds sing
Darkness back from the hills.
Something in the air, quintessence or rancor,

Makes a langur bash the skull
Of another male's progeny.
The mother tries to fight him off,
But this choreographer for Jacob

& the Angel knows defeat
Arrives in an old slam dance
& applied leverage—the Evening Star
In both eyes, something less than grace.

Utetheisa Ornatrix,
the First Goddess

Mottled with eyes, she's a snag
Of silk from a blood orange
Kimono. This moth, a proto-
Goddess, flits about as if grafted

To an uneasy moment. A little machine
Inside, she coaxes every male to deposit
Sperm, & weighs each with an unholy
Exactitude. She can correct

A mistake with metabolic
Absolution. Only the biggest is
Fertilized, & all the others grow
Into nutrients for her. Food

Defines them. Otherwise,
They depend on promiscuous
Wings to beat till their world
Turns into light & sap.

The Centaur

Shape-changer caught in the middle
Of rehearsal, here between beast
& man, like a young Chiron,
You pretend birthright,

Hoping Atalanta's arrow
Finds you on a lost path
In bloom. Yes, sometimes,
You can be loony as a drunken

Stunt man in Paradise, a bit
Of Theocritus's sad metaphysics
In your bones. One half tortures
The other for the romantic songs

Crooned at sunset. Unholy
Need & desire divide the season,
As you eat sugar from a nymph's palm,
Before she mounts & rides you into a man.

Night Ritual

The spotted hyena
Dances, her mock penis
Aimed at the moon. A mile away
A king cobra flares its hood

& strikes a lion. He kneels
Under a pendulous firmament as the venom
Takes hold. She's graceful, nimbused,
Leading her quarrelsome legion. Eyes

Flicker like stars along the timberline,
Yellow lights through grass,
& Botswana turns under their single-minded
Creed. They try to outrun luscious

Blood, till they're a tussle
Of moonlight. She's the first to sink
Teeth into the lion's belly, & yanks
With all the strength gods entrusted to her.

Lady Xoc

Thorns were woven into a cord
She pulled across her tongue,
Sacred as the gold chains
Women wear around waists

Cool against their skin.
But this love knot was a lure
With a nest of hooks. Holy
Incantations seeded the soil.

Lady Xoc knelt before Shield-
Jaguar for hundreds of years,
Clutching her braided rope
Laced like concertina,

Whose stone gaze can only be
Altered with mallet & anvil.
Until then, she'll believe blood
Can heal earth's hunger.

Lime

The victorious army marches into the city,
& not far behind tarries a throng of women
Who slept with the enemy on the edge
Of battlements. The stunned morning

Opens into a dust cloud of hooves
& drums. Some new priests cradle
Stone tablets, & others are poised
With raised mallets in a forest of defeated

Statuary. Of course, behind them
Linger the turncoats & pious
Merchants of lime. What's Greek
Is forged into Roman; what's Roman

Is hammered into a ceremony of birds
Headed east. Whatever is marble
Burns in the lime kilns because
Someone dreams of a domed bathhouse.

Ode to the Maggot

Brother of the blowfly
& godhead, you work magic
Over battlefields,
In slabs of bad pork

& flophouses. Yes, you
Go to the root of all things.
You are sound & mathematical.
Jesus Christ, you're merciless

With the truth. Ontological & lustrous,
You cast spells on beggars & kings
Behind the stone door of Caesar's tomb
Or split trench in a field of ragweed.

No decree or creed can outlaw you
As you take every living thing apart. Little
Master of earth, no one gets to heaven
Without going through you first.

Slime Molds

They're here. Among blades
Of grass, like divided cells.
Between plant & animal. Good
For nothing. In a rainstorm, spores

Glom together. Yellow-white
Pieces of a puzzle. Unable to be
Seen till united. Something
Left over from a world before—

Beyond modern reason. Primeval
Fingers reduced & multiplied
A hundredfold, the most basic
Love & need shaped them into a belief

System. The color of scrambled eggs.
Good for something we never thought
About, these pets of aliens crawl up
The Judas trees in bloom.

Sloth

If you're one of seven
Downfalls, up in your kingdom
Of mulberry leaves, there are men
Betting you aren't worth a bullet,

That your skin won't tan into a good
Wallet. As if drugged in the womb
& limboed in a honeyed languor,
By the time you open your eyes

A thousand species have lived
& died. Born on a Sunday
Morning, with old-world algae
In your long hair, a goodness

Disguised your two-toed claws
Bright as flensing knives. In this
Upside-down haven, you're reincarnated
As a fallen angel trying to go home.

Janus

When something old is grafted
To something new, as if wrested forth
By the same song, a wishbone pendulum
Sways & drags the sap down into

Half-frozen roots. Balanced
There, like *Spinario*'s head
That's at least one hundred years
Older than his body, he is

Standing & bowed before
Double doors. One foot
In fire, the other in muddy ice.
Tomorrow, yesterday, & never

Again. The new year
Gazes back to Lot's wife
Lost in a dream of summer
While the season's first snow falls.

Hermaphrodite

Sun. Moon. Hermes &
Aphrodite embrace, as a Dalí
Figure reflects a cursed body
Of water where Salmacis trapped

Hermaphroditus. Is it love
Or avarice taking him down
In a death roll among water lily
Roots? A chimera dreams

In the forest of paradox
Where anything can be fixed
In a mirrored room. Janus-
Headed alchemists fashion angels

In luciferous dusk, adding a pinch
Of bad to every pound of good,
& in the implacable dawn
God's hunger is the earthworm.

Nipples

As if my mind's double-jointed
Sometimes, I have wanted
To bow my head & kiss
My sad, stingy nipples.

I have desired music to live
Beneath the skin, with the same
Hairless ease & untamed yearning
As the *Kritios Boy* who outwitted

Time's polish. I am bowed
To questions in my head before
I was born. Hungry to kiss jubilation
Into my body, I can almost remember

When I was a girl. After the breaking
& breaking in, now these nubbins
& nips are purely aesthetic, two
Abbreviated peepholes.

Scapegoat

The alpha wolf chooses his mate
For life, & the other she-wolves
Stare at the ground. Yellowish
Light drains from notorious eyes

Of the males, stealing their first
& last sex. The pack's outcast,
The albino we humans love,
Whimpers, wags his tail,

& crawls forward on his belly.
He never sleeps at night.
After pacing down thorny grass
Where the alpha male urinated,

A shadow limps off among the trees.
Already sentenced into wilderness,
As if born wounded, he must stand
Between man & what shines.

Venus of Willendorf

She's big as a man's fist,
Big as a black-pepper shaker
Filled with gris-gris dust,
Like two fat gladiolus bulbs

Grown into a burst of twilight.
Lumpy & fertile, earthy
& egg-shaped, she's pregnant
With all the bloomy hosannas

Of love hunger. Beautiful
In a way that forces us to look
At the ground, this squat
Venus in her braided helmet

Is carved from a hunk of limestone
Shaped into a blues singer.
In her big smallness
She makes us kneel.

Body of a Dog
(Cadavere di un Cane)

He's chasing a hare.
In eleven or twelve countries
The philosophy of the hourglass
Has turned into weathered stone,

But he races the same sun
Through threadbare silhouettes.
If there were human prayers
Left, they wouldn't reach him

In Vulcan's dream come true.
Did he know when vicissitude
Eased over hills like mist or scent
Of a bitch? Given another month,

He would have made the boy
Into a very good master.
He's treed his own ghost
In a nearby poppy field.

Aftermath:
The Ruin

Stones reddened by blood
In the Roman Bath at Aquae
Sulis, what the Anglo-Saxons
Called *the work of the Giants*.

A faint city of lichen rises
When we summon the ghostly
Forefathers of Stoke Poges
& slavers. With the walls gone,

We can only imagine the *ring tank*,
The beam hooks of knotted hemp cinched
Into iron, rock hewed with spear tips
& war axes. Everything has been

Wedged into place with a boom of mud,
& no pestilence or looting could rid
This bloodline of countersigns carved
Into the stubborn dream of a mead hall.

Slaves Among Blades
of Grass

The Amazon ants dispatch
Scouts armed with mandibles
Sharp as sabers. They return
To drum each other's heads

With antennae, & then send out
Columns of warriors to surround a nest
& abduct pupae. As if made for battle,
With jaws so deadly they can't feed

Themselves, they possess slaves.
New blades of grass beaded with water
Light a subkingdom beneath
Shadowed footsteps where the sky

Meets indiscernible green of river
& jungle, in this terrain
Where a world is dismantled
To make something else look whole.

Spirit Traps

The angle at which a man
Holds up his beloved's skull
Plastered over & smoothed down
To Neolithic skin, his stare

Fixed on Jericho's night sky, is
The loneliest image I can think of
Today. Ridges of the two faces
Have been worked into calm

Seashell eyes. He sways
With the tinted globes as if cages
For scarab, believing the two bony
Sextants can shrink him to less

Than guilt. The child's bones
Surrendered to the mother's
Beneath this dirt floor
He paces like a big cat.

A Portrait of
(Self) Deception

When the grand master of folly
Turns to see if other mortals
Are looking at him & Hermaphrodite,
A hairline crack runs beneath

The Pompeian fresco, & we feel
Like children at a Saturday matinee
On the verge of shouting *Don't*
Across the river Acheron.

We see Hermaphrodite's muscle
Beneath the rounded whiteness,
& already know the outcome of this
Tussle of light & panic against

Disrobed stone. We're there
With them, where one is another,
On the precipice of Hesiod's field
As the wind sings false things true.

Stesichorus of Himera

They say he lost his sight
When he slandered Helen,
Calling Paris a schoolboy
In her faithless embrace.

Seated on the wall of Troy
With King Priam & his cronies,
She wore cloth so thin the dead
Could decipher faults & ruins,

Naming each hero's downfall.
The poet revised his story
Till she never left Attica,
Till he could almost see

The curves of a breast
Again, befuddled as a man
Cutting off a finger each day
To offer up for sacrifice.

Sex Toys

Lined up like toy soldiers
In the attitude of pillage,
They're filled with nothing but ohs
& ahs. One endless night, a tool

Of torture, & next day, a godsend
Illustration of the pleasure principle
Molded or carved into pliable mystery
& elation. Prometheus said the king of Albe

Wanted his daughter to couple with a phallus
Which appeared in his chimney, but she sent
A servant who became the mother of Romulus
& Remus. Made of aluminum or hard rubber,

As if we need something to help
Break hearts & leave slow nicks
In stony soil, these instruments
Raise temples beneath reason & skin.

Meditations
on a Thumbscrew

This can make hard men
Confess to how much water
They're made of: the saliva
It takes to polish river stones

Into a levee song. Which godhead
Did someone steal this blueprint
From in a dream? The blind prisoner
Who refused to draw a circle in dust

Around his executioner, he knew
What the Latin verb *pollere* meant
To the Greeks who said *anticheir*
(Another hand). But that was before

Ovid used the gods as punch lines,
When they were still in the trees
& hadn't yet climbed down
To curse the human thumb.

Chastity Belt

Invisible catches & secret hooks, bone
Within bone & trick locks.
If a man needs this to hold
Love in place, the master of keys

Will always bite his nails
To the quick. Tooled leather,
Laced mail, & jeweled bronze.
Before his departure over a body

Of tremulant water, he turns
The key in the lock as they kiss.
Like something alive, it sways
Beneath his armor from a gold chain

Around his neck, to the rhythm
Of galloping hooves. Two days
Later, with a dagger in his belly,
Thick fingers tear the key from his throat.

Phocylides of Miletus

Phocylides said this also: Please
Come back to bed, Love.
I didn't mean to blab
On & on, to bring into the bedroom those wormy

Epigrams. The wise men
& senators parley my wit,
But you pierced the masquerade
Without batting an eyelash.

Double-talk owns my tongue
Of sass & silver. I wanted
The ripest figs on the trees,
The sweet burden & curse,

But didn't know how to beg.
I couldn't stop running a gold thread
Beneath desire's blind stitch. No wonder,
Aphrodite, you aren't a woman anymore.

Bonsai, Golden Lotus

Grafted to composure, a courtesan
Sways like a willow, & the sap
Stuns into a fierce singing
Snipped to mourning twigs

& trained bones. Divining rod
Cut from one musical limb
& limp. Wounded into beauty,
This root-bound unblooming

Breaks midsentence & falls through
The bottom of chance. The trees stop
Limping when someone chops down a grove
To make an idea live, stealing breath

From a lotus raised out of a half sleep.
A shiver goes through hand-painted silk.
Stunted into green pleas, the whimper
& laugh grow into each other.

Envy

Icarus imitated the golden plover,
Drawn toward a blue folly
Above, looping through echoes
Of a boy's prankish laughter,

Through an airy labyrinth
Of conjecture. A lifetime
Ahead of Daedalus, with noon sun
In his eyes, he outflew the bird's

Equilibrium, wondering how this
Small creature of doubt braved
The briny trade winds. Surely,
In a fanfare of uneclipsed wings

Driven by dash & breathless style,
He could outdo the plover's soars
& dares. But he couldn't stop
Counting feathers against salty sky.

Ides of March

The wind rallies all day
With fists on doors & windows,
As St. Vitus' dance ascends
The turnstile of budding branches

Till a smoke bloom falls.
An elf's piñata on the bottom
Doorstep. Which oak rafter
Did this wasp nest cling to?

The third, the fourth? I wait
For wind to nudge a second one
Down, for it to skedaddle
From a moment wedged into eaves

Like a warning or curse throbbing
With sockets of remembered fire,
For a boy's red-tailed kite
To break free from the power line.

Aliens

We stand like Lucretius
Figuring out how one's right side
Fits into the mirror's left, just
When a whisper creeps out of wood,

Stone, water, & encompasses the sky.
Stopped in the prayer's sixth line,
We huddle amidst a throng of dogs
& sniff danger. Steven says,

"God is a postulate of the ego."
Freeways grow silent, the birds
Louder. As if awaiting a command,
We shift from foot to foot,

Hat in hand. Are thoughts
Ours? Now that we're no longer
Godlike, we can't take
Our eyes off the tumblebug.

Meditations
in a Swine Yard

A god isn't worth the salt
In our bread if we can't
Stamp our feet & shake a balled fist
At eaters of the brightest insects

On their first day here.
Sometimes we must tug him out
Into the hog's bloody mud.
His beauty is our blue

Derision, like a child banging
Her rag doll against the floor,
Calling for Daddy. A god isn't worth
A drop of water in the hell of his good

Imagination, if we can't curse
Sunsets & threaten to forsake him
In his storehouse of belladonna,
Tiger hornets, & snakebites.

The Devil's Ball

Because someone could sit
In China for so long, maybe
Imagining one hundred wild days
Of lovemaking beside a green river,

As his blade carved ivory spheres
One inside another, we named it
After the contours of our minds.
The patience of seeds in a pod

Seldom enters the metal & wood
Of our tools, & we whisper
To the stars, Time is money.
Maybe the delicate faces,

Houses, & scenes were whittled
While he watched a ginkgo
Measure the summer skies
& a lotus open three mouths of praise.

Bedazzled

A jeweled wasp stuns
A cockroach & plants an egg
Inside. In no time, easy
As fear eats into someone,

The translucent larva grows
Beneath its host's burnished
Shell. The premature stinger
Waits like a bad idea, almost

Hidden. Summertime
Breathes on a thorny leaf.
Before the new wasp breaks
Free, they are one. No longer

Fat on death's fugacity,
By tomorrow afternoon
It will cling to a window screen
Bright as Satan's lost tiepin.

The Congo Snake

Feet of petty chances, you
Came out on the other side
Of love & mercy. No one
Cares if you rise from the lower world

Or not, as something to grind up
For cat food, & even the hunger
Of gods can't wish you away.
In your cave of primordial mud,

Window through slow water,
We pray only ghosts & goblins
Look at you. The untouchables
Tattoo your image on the soles

Of their feet. The monkey
God swears you don't exist,
& in the house of good tidings
The devil is blessed before you.

Neither/Nor

Gods, with your great golden
Shields & winged feet, you
Granted me a perfect wish,
& then threw in a second one

As bonus. I didn't know
One was a blessing, the other
A curse. You know I don't care
About gold, the bright burdens

It buys. I have seen a world
Of chains & ankle bracelets,
But I never could stomach pure
Unadulterated illusion—or endless

Situation comedy. Lord, magicians
Sure can conjure an openmouthed
Crowd. One wish grew worthless
After driving the other from my door.

The Lure

The batfish hides there
At the bottom of desire.
A fleshy, wormlike lure
Dangles freely, luminescent

As a French tickler or line
From a love song personified.
Without eyes or guts, the male
Grows into the female, a Jonah

Inside a scaled-down Moby Dick.
She's bewitched among sea hair
& kelp, filled with forbearance
& a silent singing bitten in half,

In a holy world of mouths
Speaking watery reprieves
In needful hush, down where
His first breath was an open wound.

Infidelity

Zeus always introduces himself
As one who needs stitching
Back together with kisses.
Like a rock star in leather

& sapphires—conflagration
& a trick of silk falling
Between lost chances & never
Again. His disguises are almost

Mathematical, as Io & Europa
Pass from their dreams into his.
This lord of storm clouds
Is also a sun god crooning desire

& dalliance in a garden of nymphs.
Some days, he loves gloxinia,
& others, craves garlic blooms—
Hera, Aegina, & Callisto in the same song.

Ukiyo-e

We turn away from the flesh
On paper, but find ourselves
Praising the flow of feudal silk
& rice powder, as a samurai's gaze

Unfastens a windfall of blossoms
In some house of assignation
The other side of Hiroshige's forecast
Of slanted black rain. Somehow,

We face Utamaro's hairy ape
Who brandishes his penis
Like an untutored sword
At a pale maiden against indigo.

The two are brushed into a tussle
Of fire with water, a fury of silk
In a floating world, a season
Of flowered branches breaking.

Amber

The eyedropper of holy water
Didn't do the job. Night & day
He's been hunched over his microscope
After tweezering the extinct beetle

From resin. Holding up the tube
To glassy light that weighs less
Than fear, he knows a sneeze could destroy
His work. He's sure the millennial wings

Would blink open & stir
If he could find a half teaspoon
Of birth water. He can almost see
The hand that wore the Etruscan

Ring. Beneath the magnified glow
A touch of anger illuminates
A shadow. He tilts it right
& left, & the beetle swells.

Ode to Dust

It speaks when the anonymous
Tongue of each feather & leaf
Quivers, swearing that nothing's changed
As we touch tables & lampshades.

We breathe it in as if something
Is always beginning beneath the ruins
& perennials, mending skin under
The surface. Even the slow patina

Of the quietest lesson takes hold
Of Gudea's *Architectural Plans*,
Working while we sleep.
As if conjured by regret,

It lives on the imagination
Of all-night ghosts, like the worm
Brought forth from the feminine
Temples of wood & apple.

Body of a Woman
(*Cadavere di Donna*)

Here you are, still
Reposed behind glass
Like a work of art. Yes,
Body of precious aloneness,

There are times I desire you
In a lover's arms. Sometimes
I want you making fierce love,
With moans like thought bubbles

Of pleasure forever in Pompeii's
Lava & ash. Yet, other nights,
As Miles Davis plays ballads
In the background, like tonight,

There's only irony: I see
You're gazing out toward
The House of the Faun,
Waiting for someone.

Battle of
Ten Naked Men

A dance of muscle slides
Under almost see-through skin,
& the men rise out of themselves
As they swing down axes, swords,

& daggers, driven by an axle
Of light. Balanced by retreat
& each blow, they're on a carousel
Of blades that blood rides on,

Flanked by a double-woven paradise.
Did Pollaiuolo go to Turnus
For this scene? The quick
Earth pivots in this ballet

With the same sinew & torque
Verrocchio worked into Colleoni's horse.
Fighting over women or each other beneath
Thracian stars, they move as if unloved.

The Other Dying
the Life of the One

A boy is to a man as a man is . . .
No. Not you, too. Please
Tell them to put the dirt back
Into my mouth, & not to rhyme

Me with Archilochus. At first,
Each gaze was an honorable cloak.
But now they eat this wordy dust
Till I am only pirated allusion

& myth, flat as ale & sacramental
Bread left all night on a table.
I have been cooed like a coquette
To a misty canebrake where I stand

In the lonely shadows of a house
With Greek columns that is here
Only to make someone look good,
To be bartered for sexual favors.

The Citadel

They drag their latest victim
Down into clammy, sweet chemistry.
As if my presence can right a wrong,
I look on like a god

Who hasn't learned what chance
Means to the heliotrope's
Heuristic blooms. Maybe they journeyed
A lifetime to bring back their Helen,

& this is a scaled-down replica
Of Paris's nightmare. This
Troy, a citadel of blind eyes
Nearly lost inside the dome-shaped

Aquarium. They're almost vicious
As humans. A leg here, a wing
Over there. They pull each other in, half
Devoured before the fight begins.

Pride

Crowned with a feathered helmet,
Not for disguise or courtship
Dance, he looks like something
Birthed by swallowing its tail,

Woven from a selfish design
& guesswork. As if masked
With a see-through caul
From breast to hipbone,

His cold breath silvers
Panes of his hilltop house
Into a double reflection.
Silhouetted almost into a woman,

He can beg forgiveness now
As he leans against a window
Overlooking Narcissus's pond
Choked with a memory of lilies.

Remus & Romulus

They're at the eight teats
Of the Capitoline she-wolf,
Their naked adoration
Suspended in a leap

Of faith. Is she stone
Or bronze? If we lie
To ourselves long enough,
Practice works underneath

The pattern of this heft
Till flesh finds a way to rise
To a level of blame. The boys
Face each other, & we can see

Brutus's plot in the wolf's
Vulnerability, in her tarnished
Stare. Now she's only primal food
& sex, their first coup d'état.

Necropolis

Phantoms drift into each other
Till faces from Los Angeles
Form in the penumbral calm
Where beheaded Osiris guards

Rameses II's tomb. Torchlights
Jimmy the night's secret hush,
& the sarcophagi of fifty sons
Parade through afterlife & dust.

Knighted grave robbers left
Lanterns & pickaxes for curators
To hem & haw over. Nothing can
Dim the ungodly stare of Osiris

On some Hollywood mantelpiece
Beside vials of ash from Mount
St. Helens, as relentless loot
Rolls off riotous conveyor belts.

April's Fool

An armload of snapdragons
Clumped beside a ditch,
A season of promissory notes
Raising the dead for him.

He was picturing Jackie
Robinson on third, as he scored
Her name into the oak desk
With a Boy Scout knife.

No, he hadn't given April a half
Thought, not till seeing her
Yellow bicycle peened to the chrome
Grillwork of a Buick Special,

& couldn't eat for a week. Now,
Decades later, she's the reason
He never learned to drive, fell
For Beaujolais & a black clarinet.

Nightfall

Sea salt is in Elpenor's beard,
Ouzo on his breath, women left
Humming Billie & Piaf. He's good
With words, smooth as a locksmith

In a room of chastity belts.
There's always a Betty Boop
Who'd bet her life that she
Can save this cat-eyed Prometheus

From da Vinci's Emporium.
Every Saturday night someone new
Is on his arm, her low-cut gown
A school of angelfish.

Pale breasts of statues descend
With him, among sailors & beggars
At nightfall, to show how
Lust is stolen from holy bread.

The Four Evangelists

The lion, Mark—
The ox, Luke—
The eagle, John—
Ezekiel dreamt the wheel

Turning like a constellation,
A cycle of magpies, winter
To springtime. Paul shepherds them
Like a bawdy son of Horus.

If you can't trust dreams, the journey
Ends at birth. Gods invent themselves
So men & women see a few feet
Into the unknown. Sympathetic

Magic. Our desire
To prolong an orgasm, to be
Taken back to when we could
Almost talk with animals.

Acalophiles

They stole Goya's skull
& held it up to burnishing
Moonlight like a kaleidoscope,
A sparrow's nest, up to the eyes'

Slothful hunger, a peepshow
To press their faces against
The Milkmaid of Bordeaux
& *Majas on a Balcony*. Maybe,

One by one, they gazed inside
To unmask those dancers
At *The Burial of the Sardine*
& see if beauty balances the ugly,

But couldn't pull away
Once they'd heard his plea like birds
In the rafters of a basilica,
Till they were also *Saturn's Children*.

Silkworm

They made a fancy catch
For a nightgown out of me.
Fashioned into a silver hook's
Accomplice, a dumb eye

Against her skin, eager
Fingers fought each other
To unhook me, like an unkind
Thought in a man's brain.

Sometimes, I am a silk bud
Straining not to bleed open
With the rise & fall
Of her breasts. Desire

Snapped the wire hook
One night. Her own fingers.
Now, I am a little noose
Around a mother-of-pearl button.

The Seventeen-Year
Locust

There in its tiny tomb of D
NA, held in the mute loam
It is made of, earthbound
& antediluvian, each nymph

Busies itself sucking sap
From a tree root. True
As twelve solid-gold watches,
When the time comes, the locust

Tunnels open a chimney
Of light—a mere eyehole
Of dust & sap that hardens
Into mortar. On the brink

It waits for green to draw out
God's praise & lamentation.
As if a new bead for a rattle,
It clings to bark & eats itself empty.

Castrato

You've made me Little Red
Riding Hood. Mister Wolf
Has my scent on his breath,
& I've forgotten how to bluff

Shadows back into the hedgerow.
The same contralto is in my throat
Year after year. But the scalpel
Is what I remember most. Please note

This: hymns die on my tongue
Before they can heal.
Smooth as my sister's doll baby
Down there, I don't know how I feel

Or need. Entangled in so many
What-ifs. Neither north nor south.
I wish I knew how to stop women
From crying when I open my mouth.

Pan

Elizabeth, I must say,
Pan wasn't raising Cain among the reeds.
He had taken off his mask,
& was lying there, puffing ganja,

Blowing Rasta smoke rings
& nibbling on a golden mango,
When he glimpsed three naiads
Prancing beside the lily pond.

He rolled over & watched two ants
Struggle up a Sisyphean incline
With a moth. Silenus's brother
& father, scapegoat & earthly god,

He felt divided. The nymphs frolicked
As he played love & panic on his flute
Till Arcady drifted out of his head,
& then a whisper opened all the buds.

Pyramus & Thisbe

Their bodies hugged the old stone wall
Between them, like prisoners blowing smoke
Into each other's mouths through a reed
Pushed into a crack. At nine,

I didn't know delicious words
To say to a girl. Springtime
Mornings, between home & school,
My untutored hands & smile darkened

With mulberries. If I had known
How Thisbe hid beside that tree
At the tomb of Ninus, how a lion
Clawed at the scent in her lost scarf

& Pyramus found it torn to confetti,
How their suicides wounded the sap,
Maybe I wouldn't have eaten the sweet
Melancholic fruit till I grew sick.

Epithalamium

We washed away the live perfume
Of others, removed lush memories
Of their hands, trying to ignore kisses
Burning in our mouths, songs

Left in the inner ear, next
To a flowering bone. The hills
Climbed in the midnight blue distance
Were each other. Paths, detours,

& inclines dazzled us with mirages,
Chanced escapes. The city's roughhousing
Light-years away; no amount of blood red
Sirens could tear us apart,

Not till the blissful damage
Began to heal. Our beasts, a lion
& bull, slept side by side, as if born
To remove the other's curse.

The Business of
Angels

I don't know, can't say when they first
Shook hips like rock stars
& uprooted. Maybe they stole
Flight from Nike of Samothrace

& the altar of Zeus at Pergamum,
Or modeled after the winged god
On a silver coin from Peparethus.
Do you think an angel is nothing

But an idea grafted to a shadow
As monsters sprout from foreheads,
Feathered to muffle sacred blows?
I don't remember weighing a stone

With a blackbird's broken wing,
But I know when the question flew
Into my head I was standing here
At the kitchen window drying dishes.

Eros

He's on a hammock in Bangkok,
Eating succulent prawns & squid
Spiced with red pepper & lemongrass.
Hesiod's "Fairest of the deathless

Gods" can feel the fatigue syndrome
Loosen its grip in this archipelago
Of pleasures. He reads a pirated
Edition of *The Plague*. At twilight,

He'll go to the corner shop
& buy a jade brooch for Muriel
Back in Boise. He'll return
To Club Limbo. A new counterfeit

Gift dipped in fire. Eros throws
A kiss to the teenage prostitute,
& touches the wad of greenbacks
Nestled against his groin.

Complicity

Ariosto, I'm mad.
Because this isn't a one-night
Stand to sweeten an eternal
Bounty. I'm in love

With my wife in a city
Of Angelicas & Isabellas
Teaching green cockatoos
To curse in five languages

& daring men to follow danger
Into alleys elusive as Merlin's
Tomb in France. But I'm not
Ashamed to say that once

I was a goat-footed
High priest on a barge of wild roses,
Just another Lothario, a thief
& sham who was stolen blind.

May

The maypole glistens with pig fat.
Thousands of mayflies (I call them
Lovebugs) died the first hours
Against windshields, headlights,

Hoods, or sucked into the grillwork's
Wide grin. In humid dusk,
A sheet of sex hangs & bulbous bees
Nudge mayflowers till pain runs

Into pleasure. A bounty of failures
Swells with timorous maydew & mayblob,
As if something is loved beyond mercy.
Maybirds frolic in shambles of dawn

& ignite mayweed. Sweetheart,
Can I, may I? Should I stop
Undoing these seven bone-colored
Buttons too pretty to look at?

Lust

If only he could touch her,
Her name like an old wish
In the stopped weather of salt
On a snail. He longs to be

Words, juicy as passion fruit
On her tongue. He'd do anything,
Dance three days & nights
To make the most terrible gods

Rise out of ashes of the yew,
To step from the naked
Fray, to be as tender
As meat imagined off

The bluegill's pearlish
Bones. He longs to be
An orange, to feel fingernails
Run a seam through him.

When Dusk
Weighs Daybreak

I want Catullus
In every line, a barb
The sun plays for good
Luck. I need to know if iron

Tastes like laudanum
Or a woman. I already sense
What sleeps in the same flesh,
Ariadne & her half brother

Caught in the other's dream.
I want each question to fit me
Like a shiny hook, a lure
In the gullet. What it is

To look & know how much muscle
It takes to lift a green slab.
I need a Son House blues
To wear out my tongue.

Día de los Muertos

Terra-cotta shrines for loved ones
Who died to hurt us. We rehearse
Their tunes & display their favorite
Colors in a labyrinth of unwinding rooms

Through inner sancta where baroque
Gargoyles open their eyes to scare away
Evil. Plaster of Paris
& papier-mâché dusted with glitter.

We season The Last Supper
With salt brushed from bodies
Temporal & unreliable as amaranth
Scenting The Mission District.

Halloween skeletons earn the weight
Of ivory & façade, resting
Like some beautiful accident
On a dice maker's workbench.

Hydraulics

When a young man dedicates his life
To hydraulics, he can grow into a godhead
Overnight. Because *ram, pile, lift, jack,*
& pressure gauge own this man's tongue,

Hercules goes on a long vacation.
Hera's magic finds him on Saturday
Nights when he's drinking rum & Coke,
But Amazons know Hippolyta's Hollywood

& Vine. He's broken many guitars
Over the heads of bouncers. Mountains
Tremble, buildings cave, & water
Begins to drift uphill. Apollo

Arm wrestles his shadow in a dream,
As he describes the forests of Cerynitia,
& the next day the lions at the city zoo
Cover their eyes with heavy paws.

King of the Hill

After we count the fractured
Bones like notches on a gun butt,
We measure his cranium. A big brain
Doesn't mean a big heart. To heal

These wounds & balance this
Neanderthal's shattered eye socket
With an icy blue horizon, it took
More than faith to make him embrace

Medicinal herbs months away from flowers.
On his left side, Shanidar
Was blind as the paleoanthropologist
Who struts past the homeless vet

On the corner. Like in Tombstone,
Arizona, where skulls are shot with holes
Of light, if you hold this one up
You can see a new constellation.

Semantics

If you don't know the czar's
True color pallid as the light
In uranium, analogous to Siberian snows
Raven among Grotowski's *Gods of Rain*,

That each white lie tilts
The planet a fraction, can we trust you
With truths? We know it's hard
For you to say quicklime

Instead of anthracite. Black
Maria, blackguard, blackball.
Andrei, language can work a Judas
Kiss, can leach like the czar's bloody

Seed. Sometimes it's pea gravel
In a chicken's gizzard, & work days
Down to excrement, a dark luminosity
That betrays the devil in us.

Genet

Posed in a leather jacket
With four or five Black Panthers
Like a dare, the Hangman
Reflects in his eyes.

Silver studs glint like stars
On midnight water, & a black cockade's
Held up against half a chance
So the day magnifies.

He plays the galley slave,
The pimp's embellished felon.
He wishes himself into the role,
& tries to look hard as nails

To sidestep the fact that he loves
The human mind more than sex
& blood, that he's rehearsed
La Douce Mort before a blind director.

Alter Ego

Dogs & cats lick nipples
& genitalia of sleeping masters
Till the last whisper of blood
Escapes nocturnal eyes

& feet. Congenital heart
Trouble & inbred sadness.
They stalk dishes of caviar
& inherited phantoms in rhinestone

Choke chains, sweatered in harlequin
Colors. After spending
Seventeen billion on them yearly,
No wonder they kill babies

& the homeless in their sleep
Cauled with neon. Stillbirths
Sealed in bottles of formaldehyde—
Most monsters live only an hour.

The God of
Broken Things

He's in a lopsided heaven at Maggie's
Junk Shop. Objects of wood, iron, ivory,
Of veneer, lead, stone, glass, flimsy
Cardboard, of tin, brass, bronze . . .

He could go on forever fixing
Cracks, fissures, dents, fractures,
Rasping & gluing together what is
Unheard-of with what can never be

Broken or hurt beneath the architecture
Of planned obsolescence. *Objets d'art*
& bric-a-brac mended with ratty hemp.
The secret space the butterfly

Screw opens wings inside a heart
Made to slip into a dream. He browses
Gutted appliances, & knows if toenailed
Right a murderous thing is almost new.

Happenstance

Small things go wrong, line up
Like beads on a prayer necklace.
An abacus of desire, aces
On a slot machine in Gulfport,

& then a minor god finds himself
Speaking with Moloch's cocky tongue.
An airplane falls, a spaceship
Explodes in midair over paradise,

A nuclear meltdown sizzles
In the belly of a leaden calf,
& the Minotaur finds his way out
Of a classic loophole. Normal

Accident. Juice leaves a battery
& exiles us to primeval dark. Romeo
& Juliet divorce on TV, & dream aloud
Muscles they couldn't quite fit into love.

Infanticide

The old man says, All the girl babies
Killed in China rise here as women
Who date & marry men half dead
Within & dumb as clabber.

Ghostly ethereal as secret incense
In my room, they are afraid of sex
With passion. How does it feel to be
Exotic? I only know the railroads

Through the bones of my father.
But fingers can travel a breathless
Route: hair, skin, eyes, mouth, & shoe
Size. Down & up, what does that mean?

When death doesn't work, girl babies
Rise, trying to laugh themselves
Into this world, into idolatry.
They know too many ways to die.

Montage: MTV

The way the lotus pushes up
Through the watery mulch & shit,
The day outruns each character
From *The Book of the Dead*.

The heart's weighted for the Eater.
In the corner of the left eye
Three coeds sun on the grass.
Their eyes go back to Pilgrim's Point,

& two steps later, I'm the bellhop
Who serves whiskey in *Black Boy*.
But somewhere behind this summer day
Lee Morgan's trumpet pulls me

Beyond their fears & needs.
I hear Frantz Fanon's voice
Just before I unlock my front door
& slip into the arms of Sakhmet.

Isaac

Father would cut off his hands
For a voice out of the clouds,
The devil in his hall
Of trick mirrors where

Echo lives with the master
Ventriloquist. I bear a knife scar,
But still love him as a son
Should. I am his terror.

Sometimes I sleep with one eye
Open. He's made promises
Anyone with good sense knows
He can't keep. I've heard him

Slap himself across the face
Nightlong. There's an old word
For his sickness, but I can't lift
A myth off the page with my tongue.

Or, God in Godzilla

The Captain from Psyops says,
"Tydeus, if we have a mind, the body
Runs to keep up. When tail
Marries head, a beast rises,

& the battle's won without CS
Grenade, rocket, or laser beam."
In a luminous room of mock-ups
& boxy ad cameras, they sip

Bloody Marys. An icon stolen
From a pyramid grows in ice cubes
& on cereal boxes. Cartoons
& dream machines. The Captain

Sketches King Kong on a napkin
& holds it up to the towering
Light of an overhead projector,
Peering into Polyphemus's cave.

Doctor Feel-Good

He's a Laughing Buddha
With his head thrown back,
Body shaking like the Jesus
Christ in *Playboy* years ago.

If you don't sing with the cuckoo clock,
He brings in the plastic nose,
The squirt gun of red dye,
Stacks of funny books, & the rubber chicken.

The fantasy videos are for hard-core
Grumpiness & un-American
Grief. First, he tickles
The soles of your feet

Before prescribing Prozac.
He can't imagine boredom,
& says only a pretty smile
Assures margins of profit.

Gluttony

In a country of splendor & high
Ritual, in a fat land of zeros,
Sits a man with string & bone
For a stylus, hunched over his easel,

Captured by perfection.
But also afflictions live behind
Electric fences, among hedges
& a whirlwind of roses, down

To where he sits beside a gully
Pooling desires. He squints
Till the mechanical horizon is one
Shadow play against bruised sky,

Till the smoky perfume limps
Into undergrowth. He balls up
Another sheet in unblessed fingers, always
Ready to draw the thing that is all mouth.

Toxic Waste

Do they still say overseas
You can sell anything to an American?
He asks. His glass eye
Almost winks as he shifts

His prosthesis. I'm an unabridged
Fucking definition of modern war,
He used to declare to his freshmen
Before riddling them with brilliance

& sobriety. Hamlet
To Sophocles, Ma Rainey
To Emily Dickinson, Kierkegaard
To Red Cloud. Between bold sips

Of Merlot, an old burning friendship
Flares as if ten years were ten days.
An exquisite memory lives on & on:
The beautiful dead lover we share.

Shiva

He wandered nude out of Eden
Smiling at spellbound women in trees
& doorways. A breeze shook
Incense from leaves. They tore off

Their clothes, blocked his path,
& fell in the writhing dust.
They never knew so many kisses
Were stored inside their bodies.

His thick hair smelled of cedar.
He'd once worn a garland of skulls,
Dusted himself with funeral ashes,
& stood beside a river. A sacred tree,

Dark-skinned, almost African, *Supreme
Lord* in person. The wives followed
This beggar with the erect penis,
A trembling left in the lilies.

The Dark Lady

Nighttime rubs against windows
Like the same black cat
Who slinked out of language
Punched black-&-blue by fists

Of pallor. Did would-be lovers
Cross themselves when you entered
A room? Like a brunette Leda
Clothed in nothing but contradictions,

You were exposed by desire's sharp
Beak. As if words could ferry you
Into an embrace, each syllable
A worm in an apple. Dark Lady,

How did the color of eyes & hair
Mark your tongue? You, naked
As immortality, ambiguous as sea
Salt licking a man's spleen.

Umbra

I wonder if pumping iron
Seduces us back till Zeus
Banishes Hercules to Lydia
As Queen Omphale's slave

After he killed a good friend.
For a year—no, three—
He dressed in a woman's clothes
& wove on a wobbly loom

For the queen's amusement.
His lips flushed berry red
As he daydreamed revenge
Against King Eurytus, traveling

To Fire Island: a waterfall
Of satin where cross-dressers
Steal an aristocracy of garments
Woven of hex signs, of hook & eye.

Vainglory

She daydreams a D-cup.
She believes a polka-dot bikini
Will resurrect Adonis,
That he'll climb on a surfboard

& glide into her world
Of windflowers. The cosmetologist's
Song takes over her body
& transplants twelve

Years of happy amnesia.
The jester's flouncy outfit
Hugs each curve perfectly,
Till the translucent gel

Leaks from this fantasy.
A wishbone snaps. Her teeth
Chatter like ivory castanets,
& nothing stops the perpetual orgasm.

Succubus

It's happened again. He jolts awake
With her scent in his mouth,
On his big clumsy hands.
Her tongue, her lips flicker, as if

An alien has seduced him
Through autosuggestion,
& he can never touch his wife
Again. She's almost Bardot

From the neck down, a Max Ernst
Collage. A curator of the deals
We make with the dead,
He's already confessed

It isn't incestuous. But
She knows how to torture him
At 3 a.m., how to mimic the two
Doves trapped in his chimney.

A Small System

The Galápagos finch
Clutches a cactus thorn
In her beak. She works
Fast as a fencing master,

& we can almost see the brain
Grow. In a sky of orchids
Below, she spots a viper
Tonguing petals—the first

Desire. Once, what the worm
Taught us was sacred,
Serene as the beetle
Grub the bird now jabs

With her spear. Finely tuned
As a red-capped woodpecker,
She prances like God's little
Torquemada on the highest rotten branch.

Homunculus

Van Gogh's sunflowers blot out
My sky, while each cat's-eye burns
A vigil. The chief alchemist
Squeezes a dropper of love

To jump-start my heart. A voice so small
Only the watchdog hears my magnanimous
Prayer to carved intaglios. Outside
This chemical window, salamanders

& geckos are monsters. A mosquito hawk
Magnifies into a hang glider.
A honey-locust thorn
Sir Lancelot's javelin.

My ego, if crystallized, would fit
Into the eye socket of a hummingbird.
I may be less than your last thought, but,
Look, here's my thimble of gin.

Trap

I love the jagged, notched
Teeth, how it takes all my strength
To open its jaws, all one can muscle.
Its heavy chain like a leg iron,

Easily attached to a tree.
The little metal tongue
In a splayed clench, the thing
Where I hook the bait: greasy,

Scented with hunger, the morsel
Waits for an imaginary bear or bobcat.
At the edge of faith, doubtful
The trap will work,

I kneel before it. I know
It takes just a touch, a gesture,
The shadow of a bird's wing,
Everything to hold back my hand.

Ecstatic

Joy, use me like a whore.
Turn me inside out like Donne
Desired God to do with him.
Show me some muscle,

Sunlight on black stone.
Coldcock me about the head
Till I moan like a bell, low
As the one Goya could hear

Through the walls of
Quinta del Sordo.
Tie me up to the stocks those Puritans
Handled so well in Boston streets.

Don't let me down. I bet
You to use all your know-how
In one throttle. Please, good God,
Put everything into your swing.

Stalin

If he could blind his bodyguards
He would use a white-hot poker
From a biblical story. With car lights
Off, they saw him kneel under

A single star, definite as a bullet
Through a woman's pale breast.
"She left me as an enemy,"
He said a thousand times to that man

In the moon who showed him how
To tread footsteps Napoleon left.
After prisoners worked ice,
Routing a canal through an eternal

White field of loneliness, he didn't
Want anyone to remember his hands
Trembled as he placed flowers
On her snowcapped grave.

The White Hat

It rises out of a sunset
Slow as an omphalos
From submission, a hero
Cresting hills on his palomino,

Out of a denuded landscape
Whose citizens lost faith trying to coax
God out of good. Their hammers
Strike echoes of gold every eye

Lives for. Miss Kitty
Shuffles the cards. The proverbial
Gimp speaks folk wisdom, spooked
By a dead man's face on a passing train.

The white hat is an outlaw's
Cleansed by blood & the leading woman's
Good looks, & he's now a patron
Saint of precious metals.

In the Blood

Like Rimbaud in Ethiopia,
He slips on doeskin gloves
Before his hands touch trigger housings.
Cold steel burns Cosmoline & cerecloth,

As if to ignite the gunpowder
In his genes. *My great-granddaddy*
Was at the Alamo, he loves to say.
But it can't explain his lost twin brother,

The name his mother always called
In her sleep, the one now ten miles away
In the same desert, surrounded by bullion
& automatic rifles. If they met

They'd slap each other's shoulders,
Call the buyers barbarians, eat caviar
In Monte Carlo, talk about Alma in Rio,
& face each other like mirrors unsilvered.

The Procuress
(After Honthorst)

If not the old woman
Pointing to the young man,
If not the young woman's smile
Or her low-cut bodice,

If not the feather in his hat,
Or the purse in his left hand,
Perhaps it is some bluesy
Insinuation: *Jellyroll, T-*

Model Ford, & *turn my damper down.*
What's lost in translation isn't
The silence painted over: It is
The distance we must travel

To balance our loneliness
With the lute the woman holds,
A shadow of the night's refrain:
C. C. Rider, uncork my jug.

Etymology

Henry Crosby & Josephine
Bigelow lay in a friend's bed
On the ninth floor of the Hotel des
Artistes like an unframed sketch—dead—

Blaming it on black music
& dance. Jazz made them cock
The hammer & pull the trigger;
Valves of a horn sprung the lock

On chastity. Was it really lindy
Hop, Charleston, or the etymology
Of a four-letter word? Maybe
Freud's or Jung's psychology

Unclothed too much. They revised
Eighteenth-century minds with a 4/4
Beat, but it was something else that
Made their bodies beg door to door.

Speed Ball

Didn't Chet Baker know
They'd make a great white hope
Jump hoops of fire on the edge
Of midnight gigs that never happened?

Miles hipped him at The Lighthouse
About horse, said not to feel guilty
About Down Beat in '53. Chet stole
Gasoline to sniff, doctored with Beiderbecke's

Chicago style. But it wasn't long
Before he was a toothless lion
Gazing up at his face like a stranger's
Caught by tinted lens & brass. Steel

Blue stare from Oklahoma whispering for
"A kind of high that scares everyone
To death." Maybe a bop angel, Slim
Greer, pulled him from that hotel window.

A Famous Ghost

I thought happiness my birthright
& married the bone structure
In mother's dreams, his English
Impeccable. Though they sift

My ashes & swear I fought
The shadows of his lovers,
I am not Propertius's Cynthia.
Where I stand, it is still '63

& the flags are at half-mast.
I never wanted to be famous,
But couldn't lift my head off
The oven door. My last breath

Stole from his. Fumes slipped
Down like a prayer to the Cubist
In the basement. No, I'm not Hostia,
Though I unlaced a corset of stardust.

A Kind of Xenia

Did she linger in a wintry bed
Reading *Leaves of Grass*,
Stroking a pale breast
With a dreamy hand, half lost

In Whitman's operatic springtime
Of words, swept into estral hours
Like Giorgione's Venus, before
She rose to sit nude at an oak desk

& offer herself to this maestro?
Did the letter travel by horse,
Rail, by foot, for long days,
A week? A horned owl called

Night's prey in voluminous air
As her naked sighs miles away
Escaped when his fingers
Opened the fragrant paper.

Avarice

At six, she chewed off
The seven porcelain buttons
From her sister's christening gown
& hid them in a Prince Albert can

On a sill crisscrossing the house
In the spidery crawl space.
She'd weigh a peach in her hands
Till it rotted. At sixteen,

She gazed at her little brother's
June bugs pinned to a sheet of cork.
Assaying their glimmer, till she
Buried them beneath a fig tree's wide,

Green skirt. Now, twenty-six,
Locked in the beauty of her bones,
She counts eight engagement rings
At least twelve times each day.

August

At sixteen, I dreamt myself
To the swim hole, riding summer
Days, as I scythed a road
Out, leaning my body

Into the wild arc of insect
Dazzle. Right & left, yes
& no. I had an understanding
About man & tempered metal,

The old double-edged blade
Honed down to a crescent grin.
But it couldn't fit my grip
Smooth & true as a ball bat

When milkweed flowered
& surrendered. I look back,
Mad to make viny opalescence
Fall down for dusk like a woman.

Devilment

She stands in Barnes & Noble
With her left hand over her mouth,
& her right holds a thick book
Displaying an Etruscan satyr,

A king of mischief in green bronze.
Are they tipsy from afternoon
Cocktails? Bracelets & rings
Make the fluorescence sashay

Between the slow aisles. *Lord,*
Now, this is what I call a cock
Echoes & hangs over the bookshelves.
Her friend laughs till they're both

Laughing. How many evening gowns
Can outlast this story back home?
In a half dance, the satyr's left
Hoof seems to lift off the ground.

Rollerblades

Knucklehead spins on a wish & lucky
Star, dividing the city into hellbent
Circles, one improvisation to the next
Double-or-nothing dare. He grabs the bumper

Of a Yellow Cab & traverses Central Park,
Skirring & looping through rings, plugged
Into the Delfonics & Beastie Boys.
Zip, skid, & bone spindle . . .

Knucklehead hangs inside the bottom half
Of Odysseus's dreamt map to a country
Of lotus-eaters, E-mail, & goof-off.
Hugging curves beside the thieves of his image,

He ducks into a labyrinth of close
Calls. Their eyes collide. Knucklehead
Pivots, as if the four wheels of each blade
Could guillotine an apparition's last effigy.

Monkey Wrench

Balled into a cocked fist, sure
As a hammerlock, the pipe's cracked sleeve
Is sealed in corrosion. Elbow
Grease, leverage, anger, & oil,

Nothing works. The vise grip
Opens an icy mouth, dribbling
Rusty sighs. I almost give up, before
I see the wrench propped near a blowtorch

Beside the washing machine, inside my head
Like an abused blessing, awaiting the promise
& caress of an oily rag. I lie on my back
Beneath the house, among broken Nehi bottles,

Dog hair, & insect wings, as if the forces
Have been hard at work on a piecemeal angel.
Full of Christmas cake & eggnog, I squint up
At clandestine eyes in a loom of spiderwebs.

Meditations on a File

I weigh you, a minute in each hand,
With the sun & a woman's perfume
In my senses, a need to smooth
Everything down. You belong

To a dead man, made to fit
A keyhole of metal to search
For light, to rasp burrs off
In slivers thin as hair, true

Only to slanted grooves cut
Across your tempered spine.
I'd laugh when my father said
Rat-tail. Now, slim as hope

& solid as remorse
In your red mausoleum,
Whenever I touch you
I crave something hard.

The God of
Land Mines

He sits on a royal purple cushion
Like a titanic egg. Dogs whimper
& drag themselves on all fours through dirt
When a breeze stirs his sweet perfume.

He looks like a legless, armless
Humpty-Dumpty, & if someone waves
A photo of an amputee outside the Imperial
Palace in Hue, he'd never blink.

When he thinks *doors*, they swing open.
When dust gushes on the horizon
His face is a mouthless smile.
He can't stop loving steel.

He's oblong & smooth as a watermelon.
The contracts arrive already signed.
Lately, he feels like seeds in a jar,
Swollen with something missing.

Betrayals

One winter in San Juan
I loved one of Raphael's *Three
Graces*, as we sipped rum & Cokes
In the shadows of La Perla.

The way Picasso didn't know Apollinaire,
She strolled into El Primitivo
With her parents from Chicago,
A warning in the same translucent blue dress.

Our eyes couldn't meet, as if I were born dead
As an Iberian statuette stolen from the Louvre—
A piece Picasso knew how to break down
& crawl inside to sketch his way out.

Not knowing such sympathetic magic,
I was young & black, with a heart
Dumb as Apollinaire's, daydreaming
My sperm inside her all afternoon.

Curator of
Kosinski's Mask

Maybe he thought gods
Would gaze back through these eyeholes
Of leather soft as Leda,
Smoother than vellum.

He said, "Life, here's Death
With his orphic grin."
In the glass case is Mirth,
Over here Metamorphosis.

This is Quintus Roselus.
He called it "Beauty
Turned inside out
By what is seen."

Here's my favorite, *The Plastic
Bag.* Look how one mask fits
Inside another, how they kiss
Away each other's fear.

Postscript
to a Summer Night

As if he'd stood too long facing
A pharaoh in the Temple of Karnak
Or Hermes of Siphnos, one night
J. R. Midas copied his penis

On the company's Xerox machine,
Lying across a bed of hot light.
He was thirty-three, still half
Invincible, & scribbled on each: *I am*

On fire with love, & all the more fire
Because I am rejected . . . He x-ed out
Galatea, & wrote in names of the two
New district managers: *Melissa*, *Amy*

Lou. He hung his coat & tie on a hook,
Then strolled down to the docks
& walked under an orange moon
Till his clothes turned to rags.

September

Today, somewhere, a man
In his early seventies is lost
In a cluster of hills at dusk,
Kneeling beside a huckleberry bush.

It's been six—no, seven—days
Since he stood at his kitchen window
Gazing out toward this summit
As Armstrong's "Gully Low Blues"

Played on his Philco, hoping
The hot brass would undercut
The couple's techno & punk rock
In the basement. Two days ago,

He ate the last trail mix & beef
Jerky. Now, with a blues note in his head,
He nuzzles the berried branches
To his mouth, like a young deer.

The God of
Variables

He nudges me out of Shangri-La
Collaged with Victoria's Secret,
As he gazes down like Socrates,
Saying, *Now, suppose Nicole*

Simpson weighed 300 pounds
Or if she'd been a Dorothy
Dandridge? I shake my head
& his notes blur into Dow Jones.

Okay. Now let's drift back
To Emmett Till, to a wolf
Whistle in a town called Money,
To a night swollen with bullfrogs

& honeysuckle. A cotton-gin wheel
Spins on the Tallahatchie. He pokes me
With a blue finger. *Now, if Louise*
Woodward was a descendant of Sancho—

Catwalk

Every sidewalk's a treadmill
Meandering along a ripple & strut
Of flesh beneath the metaphysics
Of cloth or lack of. Somewhere

A hurricane off the coast of Africa
Heads to the Caribbean, to the Gulf . . .
Can jeans & short dresses take our minds
Off magma beneath the fox-trot & tango,

Runaway asteroids jiggling bones
Like worry beads on photo shoots?
But the gods are never caught
Crawling from top-notch machines,

& memory's broken skull lingers
On every corner where dogs are
Bred into distinction & beauty is
Praised down to the worm in the ark.

Rave

He says, You have to know, huh?
Well, I listen to it because
I can't stumble into bliss,
Can't kill myself with sugar.

It makes my head hurt, she says.
I feel plugged into a box of wires
Dangling loose. Sampled rigmarole
In a gallery of Donatien-Alphonse-

François. He sits in the booth
Beside her, shaking his head.
You don't hear right, he says.
The re-echo has you on tenterhooks.

I love you. But that vociferous
Thump-thump sounds like a flywheel
Rattling around in an unbolted nogginbox,
& I'm ready to kill somebody, she says.

St. Valentine's Day

Lovers argue so they can kiss
& feed each other chocolates
All day, & then fall for profiles
Of Daphnis between Snug Harbor

& the AIDS clinic.
Mardi Gras beads mottle
Sidewalks & Dixie Crab
Boil seethes from cypress walls.

Swift hands of bacchanal clocks
Turn as two boys dance,
Dressed in hair shirts
On Elysian Fields Avenue.

They work hypnosis by running
Through a gauntlet of twilight,
Discarded ribbons & cards, lashing
Passersby with swathes of goatskin.

Curanderismo

Dear, I roll this duck egg
Over your breasts to steal
The poison, old troubles,
& lamentation. The angry cells

Will sprout in this sacrifice
That now takes on your burdens
& pleas. The mystery of gods
Lives on our bodies. I want you

To take this icon, my dear,
Wrap it in a silk garment,
& bury it thirty-three paces
Among the trees. Disbelief

Can't change what's happened here
Tonight, with these bad omens
Zonked, & I can't think ugly
Since I deal in cosmic stuff.

Necrophilia

Those years he watched her
Intently as the Frog Prince,
Did he know a star would fall
& pierce like a voodoo doll?

Her father owns the car lot, bank,
Supermarket, gas station, & floral shop.
When he was a teenager in a blizzard
Of white sheets, he'd play dead so long

Only her face behind his eyelids
Would bring him back. The first kiss
Was light as the one he'd given his mother
In the coffin. Now, Sleeping Beauty

Trembles under his touch. Only a man
With his tongue cut out can tell us
What this means, all these petals
Shaken to the floor like snow.

Negative Capability

The honeysuckle vines are certain
They'll be here tomorrow morning,
Unhushed scent reaching into next month,
As I rest the scythe against a stump

To sharpen the curved blade.
Their green surety. My uncertainty:
That pain in the chest could return
In the middle of this job, a ferryman

Singing *One more river to cross.*
A miracle defines itself. I love
What doesn't reveal every seam,
Every droplet—when doubt owns tongue

& clitoris, heart & penis. I love
Mystery, & hope I never touch naked
Threads of reason to answer the slimy,
Clueless snout probing the dark.

The Goddess of
Quotas

In my alabaster skin, I don't
Possess a photographic memory
But I can still see Du Bois
At the back of a bus, see

Little side windows in shops
Sliding open like guillotines
Years after I first dated
The god of variables. *No Dogs*

Kikes Dagos Spics Niggers,
A sign said. I'm not dust yet,
But I remember ballot boxes
& want ads too, August Sundays

When the boys dissected Eden
& evil-eyed us girls. Friend,
My heart was divided by a rope
That halved a rock & roll dance hall.

Anger

We can cut out Nemesis's tongue
By omission or simple analysis.
Doesn't this sin have to marry
Another, like a wishbone

Worked into meat, to grow
Deadly? Snared within
The blood's quick night,
Our old gods made of sex

& wit, of nitrate & titanium,
Hurl midnight thunderbolts
& lightning. Are we here
Because they must question

Every death in an alley,
Every meltdown? We know
We wouldn't be much, if thorns
Didn't drive light into wet blooms.

October

Half of summer, at the lonely
Wooded edge you lingered.
Now, with that wet nose
Pressed to the windowpane,

I fear for you. In changing
Coat, your antlers a crime.
I say *Arrow & rifle slug*,
But you keep edging closer.

I wish you understood salt licks
& blinds. If you were in northern
Mexico, not in New Jersey
Where the leaves fake blood,

Praise would be a Tarahumara
Chasing you till a heart detonates
Shadows, till Actaeon's voice is
Surrounded by his baying hounds.

Outside Gethsemane

Ghosts in walls keep words alive.
Post-this & post-that. Herme-
Neutics & boredom pick each bone
Clean. Speck & spectacle. (Id)

Eas mutate till dollar signs
Cannibalize memories, dangling
Empty hulls in slatted stalls
Of bartered light. The heart

Caves in when we shimmy up scales
To sell each other by the pound.
Quid, ducat, peso, yen, & cowrie
Shell. Cans of air. Pet Rocks.

Death chews off a finger to show
What it is made of. Vowels dribble
Pinfeathers. We nibble on a spine
To force the thing to howl, to crawl.

Philosophers, Incorporated

Curators of midnight
Desires, we still need
You as much as hemlock
& larkspur, sex

& arpeggios. To answer
The hermit thrush & worm
We fill every mystery
With your names. Divine

Scapegoats & voyeurs,
At whose feet we cast
Conceit, what we now see
Reflected in each other's eyes

Scares us. Whoever you are,
Prophets or crapshooters, please
Watch us deep as the gyrfalcon
Gazes upon the dozing diamondback.

The Polecat

Thanks for your warning
Along the chilly hedgerow.
I have seen dogs roll in the dust
& run in circles, nudge the hemlock,

Trying to shake off the essence
Of you. Your scent rises up
Through the living-room floorboards,
The odor of fear from saw vines

& cockleburs. I fold both hands
Into a mask. Those days, in love,
Protesting for the spotted owl
Among my last good witnesses,

I remember a sheriff aiming pepper gas.
Praised or damned, it depends where
We stand, little terrorist
Of the stink bomb.

Crow Lingo

Can you be up to any good
Grouped into a shadow against Venus,
Congregated on power lines around
The edges of cornfields?

Luck. Curse. A wedding.
Death. I have seen you peck
Pomegranates & then cawcawcaw
Till hornets rise from purple flesh

& juice. I know you're plotting
An overthrow of the government
Of sparrows & jays, as the high council
Of golden orioles shiver among maple

& cottonwood. Your language
Of passwords has no songs,
No redemption in wet feathers
Slicked back, a crook's iridescent hair.

Yesteryear

The sheriff slides a black knob
Of polished oak from its blue
Velvet box, smooth
As a bull's horn.

His wife of twenty-two years
Sighs, gazing out at a jaundiced
Moon. He says, "Yeah, I truncated
The bastard's balls with my billy club."

As if weighing good & bad, he holds
A breast in each hand. "The big one,
The tough sonuvabitch, we took him
For a long ride in the graveyard."

His right hand slides down
To her wet sadness. Somewhere
A hoot owl calls. Somewhere
A moan opens a mouth, the eyes of many gods.

Meditations
on an Olmec Head

Along stations of the sword,
Cross, & plumed serpent,
Someplace between Xochipala
& here, a flotilla of boats

Nudges beyond monolithic green.
As if from among unlit mug shots
In a logbook of wanted posters
Chained to a post office wall,

This figure rises at daybreak
With *gumbo* & *yam* on the lips,
A stone that refuses to be
Dated. Big-shouldered

& awesome, the towering face
In a hemispherical helmet
Grows into a Detroit Lion,
A Chicago Bear on a billboard.

The Devil's Workshop

The master craftsman sits like Rodin's
Thinker, surrounded by his cosmic tools,
Experimenting with the greenhouse effect
& acid rain. A great uncertainty

Plagues him. Some hard questions
Wound the air. Yesterday afternoon
Children marched with a rainbow
Of placards. Perhaps he can create

A few suicides with his new computer
Virus. Something has gone wrong
In the shop, because the old gods
Of serpentine earthquakes & floods

Are having more fun than he is
In his laboratory of night sweats
& ethnic weapons. Lovers smile
As Cupid loads a blowgun with thorns.

Mud

She works in the corner of the porch
Where a trumpet vine crawls up to falling
Light. There's always some solitary
Bridge to cross. Right hand

& left hand. The dirt dauber
Shapes a divided cell
Out of everything she knows,
Back & forth between the ditch.

I could take a stick & play
God. Soldier. Sadist. Nosing
Mud into place, she hums the world's
Smallest motor. Later, each larva

Quivers like bait on a hook . . . spermatozoa
Clustered in a song of clay. So small
Only the insignificance can begin
To fill the afternoon.

The God of
Variables Laments

The other day I was dining out
With You Know Who, saying,
Don't worry if they call you PC
Lady, because they only want you

To question your heart till it's nothing
But a pinch of rock salt. The Master
Of Weights & Balances strolled over
To our table, favoring his right foot,

& stood glowering at us. I still
See his hate letters to Hank Aaron.
Finally, I said, Hi, Frank.
He said, Don't care what you say,

Property values are up. Manifest
Destiny is our liturgy. The god-
Forsaken moon is ours, too, & you
Can't teach wood not to worship fire.

Potions

The old woman made mint
Candy for the children
Who'd bolt through her front door,
Silhouettes of the great blue

Heron. She sold ten-dollar potions
From a half-lit kitchen. Chinese boxes
Furnished with fliers & sinkers. Sassafras
& lizard tongues. They'd walk out

Of the woods or drive in from cities,
Clutching lovesick dollar bills
At a side door that opened beside
A chinaberry tree. Did their eyes

Doubt under Orion as voices
Of the dead spoke? They carried
Photos, locks of hair, nail clippings,
& the first three words of a wish.

Incubus

Her beige uniform's crumpled
At the foot of a motel bed
After a ghost of the navigator's cologne
Followed her past the cockpit.

Pensacola to L.A. She plays dead.
Winged tattoos on her breasts
Quiver like the night she lost
The baby. Heat lightning strobes

The venetian blinds, a moan
Works deeper beneath the weight
Of sleep, & the scent of asphodel
Unblesses the air. Nude

Against pale sheets, she
Can feel the throb of an evening
In D.C. when the beauty mark
Vanished from her left cheek.

Vatsyayana

I don't wish to deflower you on Avenue A
Beneath a quarter moon, a glimpse of Shiva
Naked among river trees in the brain,
Cursing your alibis for Indra

& King Dandakya. I detest
Your caste of color schemes
Where lingam lords over yoni.
I bow to the Peacock's Claw,

The Leap of the Hare,
The Leaf of the Blue Lotus.
After my braided belt of thorns
We can rehearse the Coral & Jewel,

The Pair of Pincers,
The Chasing of the Sparrow,
& the Bite of the Wild Boar
As wings beat a golden cage raw.

Euphony

Hands make love to thigh, breast, clavicle,
Willed to each other, to the keyboard—
Searching the whole forest of compromises
Till the soft engine kicks in, running

On honey. Dissonance worked
Into harmony, evenhanded
As Art Tatum's plea to the keys.
Like a woman & man who have lived

A long time together, they know how
To keep the song alive. Wordless
Epics into the cold night, keepers
Of the fire—the right hand lifts

Like the ghost of a sparrow
& the left uses every motionless muscle.
Notes divide, balancing each other,
Love & hate tattooed on the fingers.

The Goddess of
Quotas Laments

George Wallace is dead.
Few recant as he did, dropping
Skeins & masks, but I still see
The army of dragon's teeth

He planted like Cadmus of Tyre.
Fists of oaks clutch barbed wire.
How many replicas of him relume,
Wheedling east & west, here

To Kingdom Come, in vernal
Valleys & on igneous hillocks
That overlook god knows where?
I wish I knew why hatemongers

Drift to the most gorgeous
Spots on earth. I have watched
Choke vines & sunlight in cahoots,
Edging toward a cornered begonia.

November's Nocturne

A rainstorm slants into an icy
Wedge. Windows & doors whine
A jam session of bedsprings
In love's deep twilight. Twigs

Quiver. Black notes & hieroglyphics.
Every branch wrestles, denuding
The woods as a woman passes naked
Before panes no longer hidden.

Our old selves return like a neighbor
Released from a prison of restless
Blood red leaves. The houses ease
Closer. A glimpse. Here & there

A breast, a mouth, something
Almost in focus, slow as *Venus
Genetrix*'s drapery cut in stone: Before
Lingers in the eyes of a redbird.

Ode to the Raccoon

I have witnessed you
Wash your paws at the altar
Of your moony reflection
Halved by a dogwood.

People say grace over you
In the backwoods—garnished
With sweet potatoes & red peppers.
I have seen you fold paws across

Ringed eyes to shield out
Flashlights, as stout men
Climbed oaks to shake you down
For the dogs. Raised on hind legs,

With fruity entrails perfuming
The cold night air, you fought
Till the men kicked the dogs off
To save you for their blessings.

Heresy

Yes, blood lit the sword
East & West to divide
Gods from Homo sapiens.
No, it wasn't the penis

Pharisees wished abridged
& amputated. That season
Tongues rotted like fat figs
On broken branches. Pelagian

Wit could cost a man his head.
Women were already banished
From the pulpit, & their songs
Held only an after-scent of myrrh.

Some sculpted lies & dripped gold
Into them. Others saw burning pyres
& said Free Will couldn't live
In a doll's body, termites in the godhead.

Printed in the USA
CPSIA information can be obtained
at www.ICGtesting.com
LVHW091146150724
785511LV00005B/566